Neil deGrasse TYSON

Pete DiPrimio

PURPLE TOAD
PUBLISHING

Printing   1   2   3   4   5   6   7   8   9

A Beacon Biography

Big Time Rush
Carly Rae Jepsen
Drake
Harry Styles of One Direction
Jennifer Lawrence
Kevin Durant
Lorde
Markus "Notch" Persson, Creator of *Minecraft*
Neil deGrasse Tyson
Peyton Manning
Robert Griffin III (RG3)

Publisher's Cataloging-in-Publication Data
DiPrimio, Pete.
   Neil deGrasse Tyson / written by Pete DiPrimio.
     p. cm.
        Includes bibliographic references and index.
        ISBN 9781624690907
1. Tyson, Neil deGrasse—Juvenile literature. 2. Astrophysicists—United States—Biography—Juvenile literature. I. Series: Beacon Biographies Collection Two.
   QB460 2015
   523.01092
                                   Library of Congress Control Number: 2014937123

eBook ISBN: 9781624690914

ABOUT THE AUTHOR: Pete DiPrimio is an award-winning Indiana sports writer and columnist, a long-time freelance writer with three published sports books pertaining to Indiana University, and a veteran children's author with nearly 20 published books. He's also a fitness instructor and has been a journalism adjunct lecturer.

PUBLISHER'S NOTE: The data in this book has been researched in depth, and to the best of our knowledge is factual. Although every measure is taken to give an accurate account, Purple Toad Publishing makes no warranty of the accuracy of the information and is not liable for damages caused by inaccuracies. This story has not been authorized or endorsed by Neil deGrasse Tyson.

CONTENTS

Neil deGrasse Tyson brings space to Earth. Here he is shown with Pluto and its largest moon Charon.

"How could he?" people asked. "Why would Neil deGrasse Tyson be
so mean?"

Students wrote letters begging him to change it back. Even some
scientists wondered what Tyson, one of the world's most famous
astrophysicists, was thinking.

What caused all the fuss?

Tyson had started a movement that eventually kicked Pluto out
as a planet. After almost eighty years of science saying our Solar
System had nine planets, it would now have eight.

Pluto was . . . a dwarf.

"Don't blame me for the death of Pluto," Tyson said. "All I did
was drive the getaway car." The real killer, he added, was astronomer
Mike Brown, author of *How I Killed Pluto and Why It Had It
Coming.*

First, a little background.

Scientist Clyde W. Tombaugh from the Lowell Observatory in
Flagstaff, Arizona, discovered Pluto in 1930. At first, he called it
Planet X. Eventually, it was named Pluto, thanks to a suggestion by
an eleven-year-old girl in England. It was named for the Roman god
of the Underworld, not the Disney character.

In 1992, astronomers discovered the Kuiper Belt, which is a band of icy, rocky objects at the edge of the Solar System, right where Pluto was discovered. Most were smaller than Pluto, but some were about the same size. Tyson quickly realized Pluto resembled them more than it did a planet. By then he was the director of the New York's Rose Center for Earth and Space at Hayden Planetarium. In 2000, he changed the Solar System display from nine to eight planets. A *New York Times* reporter wrote a story about it. Some astronomers said Tyson was being, well, silly. Upset people wrote angry letters.

Pluto is a planet, they said. No way, Tyson responded.

More and more astronomers began agreeing with Tyson. Finally, in 2005, Caltech astronomer Mike Brown and his team found a Kuiper Belt object bigger and farther away from the Sun than Pluto. They called it Eris. It was not, they said, a planet.

In 2006, the International Astronomical Union did what would once have been unthinkable: they classified Pluto as a dwarf planet, just another object in the Kuiper Belt. The Solar System really did have only eight planets.

Still, people were upset. They blamed Tyson.

One elementary student wrote to Tyson, "Some people like Pluto. If it doesn't exist, then they don't have a favorite planet."

Another student wrote, "I think Pluto is a planet. Why do you no longer think Pluto is a planet? I do not like your answer. Pluto is my favorite planet!!! You are going to have to take all the books away and change them. PLUTO IS A PLANET!!!!!!!"

Still, Tyson didn't back down. Pluto wasn't a planet. It was too small. It was more ice than rock. If it was as close to the Sun as Earth was, the ice would melt and a tail of debris would stream behind it, like a comet.

In fact, Tyson told a group of students during a lecture, it would be "The King of Comets."

He said if the planet Saturn were the size of a regular car, Pluto would be the size of a Matchbox car. Our Solar System has six moons bigger than Pluto, including the Earth's moon.

To understand more about Pluto, NASA sent a spacecraft, called *New Horizons* to study this faraway rock.

Planet or dwarf, Pluto still fascinates people. NASA, the U.S. space agency, has sent its *New Horizons* spacecraft to study Pluto. The probe was set to reach Pluto in 2015 and take photos of its surface.

Tyson, meanwhile, continues talking about Pluto and outer space. He pushes for more funding for the space program because, he says, it's so important to our country. He has been on many TV shows. He has hosted his own radio show, called *StarTalk Radio.* He has become so famous, *People* magazine once called him "The Sexiest Astrophysicist Alive." In 2013, he had more than 1.5 million followers on his Twitter account. He has an asteroid named after him: 13123 Tyson. *TIME* magazine once listed him as one of the 100 most influential people in the world. *Discover* magazine called him one of the 50 Best Brains in Science. He has received eighteen honorary doctorates, plus the NASA Distinguished Public Service Medal, the highest award given by NASA to a non-government citizen.

Tyson's fame comes with a purpose.

"My hope is by being visible, I am opening doors so that people better than I am, who might never even have thought they could do this, will be revealed to modern society."

What does that mean?

Let's take a look.

The Comet Kohoutek never lit up the sky as some scientists predicted, but it was bright enough to be visible. In January 1974, teenaged Neil deGrasse Tyson went to California's Mojave Desert for an astronomy camp to get a better look.

End of the World?
No Way!

Was the world about to end? No way, Tyson said. He was fourteen years old in 1973 and didn't believe what some religious groups were saying—that Comet Kohoutek, which would get close enough for people to see without a telescope, would destroy Earth.

Tyson was in California's Mojave Desert, far from his New York home, as part of an astronomy camp to get a good look at Kohoutek. For one month he made a lot of observations, took a lot of notes, and tried taking pictures of Kohoutek's long and not-so-bright tail.

The world didn't end, and for most, Kohoutek proved to be less than spectacular. But when Tyson finished the camp, he knew for certain what he had been thinking about for the last five years: He was going to be an astrophysicist.

Tyson was born on October 5, 1958, in New York City, to a family that loved learning. His father, Cyril, was a sociologist and human resource commissioner for New York City. His mother, Sunchita, was a gerontologist: she studied the science of aging. Tyson also had a younger sister, Lynn (who became a Dell computer company executive), and an older brother, Stephen.

Tyson's first glimpse of the wonder of outer space came when he was nine years old. He lived close to the American Museum of

Natural History's Hayden Planetarium in New York. There, on the ceiling, he saw the Milky Way, which is Earth's galaxy. It was way more spectacular than what he could see from atop Brooklyn's Skyview Apartments, where he was living.

He was fascinated. He had to know more. A year later, in July 1969, when astronaut Neil Armstrong became the first person to walk on the moon, Tyson couldn't learn fast enough.

Shortly after that, Tyson used a borrowed pair of binoculars to gaze at the sky from his apartment building's roof. He still couldn't see the Milky Way, but he could see how cool the moon was. If only he had something more powerful to use.

For his twelfth birthday, his parents gave him the perfect present—a 2.4-inch telescope, plus a solar projection screen. Soon, he got a bigger telescope that included an electric clock for tracking stars. He would roam the apartment roof, observing and recording.

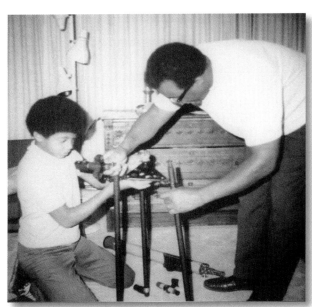

What did space really look like? Tyson needed a telescope to see, and when he was 12, his parents got him one. His father, Cyril, helped him put it together.

Sometimes, people would see a person up there and call the police. The police soon became very familiar with this bright boy with an even brighter future.

Because city lights blocked out many of the stars, Tyson went to the country, just like famous Italian astronomer Galileo had done hundreds of years before. There it was dark enough to really see what space was all about.

Tyson also began taking classes at the Hayden Planetarium. In 1973, the international race to the stars began. NASA launched a space probe called *Pioneer 11* that would explore the asteroid belt between Jupiter and Saturn, and then continue beyond. Carl Sagan, perhaps the world's most famous astronomer, talked NASA into putting a plaque on *Pioneer* with all sorts of information about Earth and its people—just in case aliens from another world would one day find it.

Tyson did so well in his classes that he began teaching adults. He loved it. He later wrote that for him, "talking about the universe was like breathing."

Tyson was also a good athlete. In 1976, as a senior at the Bronx High School of Science, he was a wrestling team captain. When it came time to pick a college, Tyson focused on the school with the best astronomy program. For him, that meant Harvard University; but Sagan tried to convince him to go to Cornell. Sagan taught at Cornell, and the admissions office there forwarded him Tyson's very passionate application. Sagan sent him a personal invitation to tour the campus, and then met him on a snowy Saturday to show him around.

Meanwhile, Tyson's high school counselor thought he should focus on colleges with good wrestling programs. "Never mind that Harvard was the leading institution in astrophysics and I had this burning desire to be an astrophysicist," Tyson said in an interview with *Ebony* magazine. "She [the counselor] could only see me in the stereotypical role of black male athlete."

Tyson wouldn't let that attitude discourage him. "My interest in the field of study was so strong and my reserves of energy so deep that I always knew I could out-fight forces that were trying to turn me away."

He was accepted at Harvard and made his decision. He headed to Cambridge, Massachusetts.

At Harvard, Tyson proved he could be a very good athlete (he was on the rowing team and also wrestled) as well as a very good student.

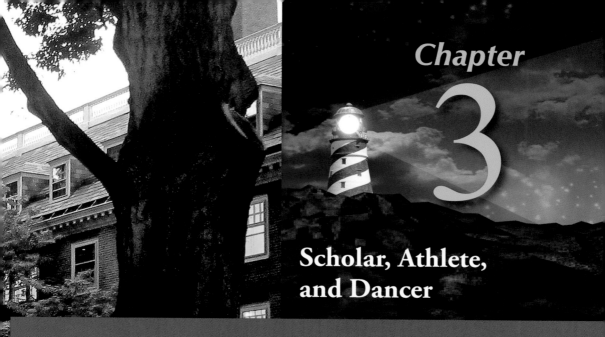

Chapter 3

Scholar, Athlete, and Dancer

After he received his bachelor's degree from Harvard, Tyson received a master's degree from University of Texas, and then he began working toward his doctorate in astrophysics. He was a smart man on the move, in part because he didn't believe in limits.

All the while, he received weird questions about what was going on in the sky. Strange lights, exploding stars, eerie objects, a glow that didn't seem quite right—it didn't matter. Tyson was the answer guy. He answered questions on campus, and he began publishing his answers to readers' questions in *StarDate* magazine.

As a Harvard freshman, he was on the rowing team. As a senior, he lettered in wrestling. And when he started graduate work at the University of Texas, he joined the dance team. He helped the team win a gold medal at a national tournament in the International Latin Ballroom style. Meanwhile, he explored the city of Austin by bicycle. When he could squeeze in free time, Tyson tutored prisoners in math.

In a class on relativity at Texas, he met Alice Young. She was very smart, getting her PhD in mathematical physics and becoming a computer programmer. In 1988, they married. They would eventually have two children—Miranda and Travis.

But there were some drawbacks to living in Texas. Tyson sometimes experienced discrimination. He wondered why university police would sometimes stop and question him as he was about to enter the physics building, but never while going to the gym.

Academically, he wasn't making fast enough progress on his dissertation. Professors encouraged him to try another career. Finally, advisers, in essence, flunked him.

It was time to move on.

So Tyson transferred to Columbia University in New York City. He was close to home and family and even though he didn't yet know it, he was close to a future job.

Eventually, he became the astrophysicist that New York reporters called when the night sky turned strange. Why? Tyson was smart, funny, and interesting and was comfortable in interviews and in front of a camera.

After getting his PhD in 1991, he accepted a research job at Princeton University.

In the late 1980s, he had taken all the columns he'd written for *StarDate* and turned them into his first book, *Merlin's Tour of the Universe.* The book got the attention of officials at New York's Hayden Planetarium, where Tyson had spent so much of his childhood. The planetarium was nearly sixty years old. It needed a new look and approach. Officials wanted a young, energetic director with vision. They thought Tyson would be perfect for the job, but he wasn't quite ready to accept.

He kept his position at Princeton while joining the Hayden Planetarium science department. One of his main jobs was helping to redesign the facility. That included getting new exhibits.

Things really picked up when Frederick P. Rose, a wealthy New York businessman, gave $20 million to finish the renovation and boost the astrophysics department. That was enough for Tyson. In 1996, at the age of 38, he became the director of Hayden Planetarium's Frederick P. Rose Center.

Few places can show you what outer space is really like better than the Rose Center at Hayden Planetarium.

The Rose Center opened in 2000 and was a big hit, full of state-of-the-art exhibits and designs.

But Tyson did a lot more than just run a neat planetarium. He did research on star formation, exploding stars, dwarf galaxies, and the Milky Way. And he got involved with Pluto.

In 2001, President George W. Bush appointed Tyson to a twelve-member commission that looked at where the United States' space program should go. The commission wrote a report that was sent to Congress. It was designed to push for more space exploration as well as transportation and national security.

In 2004, President Bush appointed Tyson to serve on a nine-member commission for U.S. Space Exploration Policy. It was called the Moon, Mars and Beyond Commission.

Two years later, Tyson joined NASA's advisory council to help the space agency best use its budget to explore space. He had a lot of ideas. Some of them were serious. Some were fun. And thanks to his position and visibility, he could make them happen.

Tyson became a comic book hero to help Superman find his home planet of Krypton in a 2012 graphic novel by DC Comics.

Chapter 4

Finding Krypton

Krypton was out there. Superman's home planet existed in the fictional world of DC Comics, and it was time for him to find it.

Who could help him? Neil deGrasse Tyson.

Not only did Tyson deliver to the DC Comic request, he found himself as a comic book character in the same 2012 graphic novel—Action Comics Superman #14, *Star Light, Star Bright*—with Superman.

"As a native of Metropolis, I was delighted to help Superman, who has done so much for my city over all these years," Tyson said in a statement. "And it's clear that if he weren't a superhero, he would have made quite an astrophysicist."

For the record, Tyson found Krypton 27.1 light-years from Earth. It is in the southern constellation Corvus (The Crow) and orbits the red dwarf star LHS 2520. That's a smaller, cooler star than the Sun.

Superman was born on Krypton. He was just a baby when his father, Jor-El, who realized Krypton was about to be destroyed, sent him to Earth. Superman landed in Kansas, where he was found by a farmer and his wife and raised as Clark Kent.

"This is a major milestone in the Superman mythos that gives our super hero a place in the universe," DC Entertainment co-publisher

Dan DiDio said in a statement. "Now fans will be able to look up at the night sky and say, 'That's where Superman was born.' "

To find LHS 2520 with a telescope, here are the coordinates:

Right Ascension: 12 hours 10 minutes 5.77 seconds
Declination: −15 degrees 4 minutes 17.9 seconds
Proper Motion: 0.76 arc seconds per year, along 172.94 degrees
from due north

Tyson's fame goes way beyond comic books. He hosted a radio talk show about outer space called *Star Talk Radio.* The idea was to combine science and humor, which is why comedians Lynne Koplitz, Chuck Nice, and Leighann Lord, plus famous guests, helped him host. Topics included space travel, aliens, the Big Bang (a theory about how our universe was created), the environment, and more.

Or, as Tyson put it, "[We'll explore] everything under the sun; or, rather, under the universe!"

For instance, one show was called "I Robot." Stephen Gorevan, one of the founders of Honeybee Robotics, talked about how we use robots, including a robot inchworm that rolls through steam pipes under New York. When the robot finds a hole, it welds it shut.

Tyson has appeared in a lot of TV shows. He hosted the PBS miniseries *Nova* and appeared regularly on the History Channel's *The Universe.* He's also been on CNN and talk shows such as *The Tonight Show* with Jay Leno, *The Daily Show* with Jon Stewart, *The Colbert Report,* and *Late Night with Conan O'Brien.* In 2014, the Fox network launched a 21st century version of the classic 1970s science show *COSMOS* starring Tyson. It was, originally hosted by Carl Sagan.

Tyson continues to publish popular astronomy books. He has also written for dozens of professional publications.

Tyson has over 1.5 million followers on Twitter. He uses his account to give his thoughts on science, the world, and so much more.

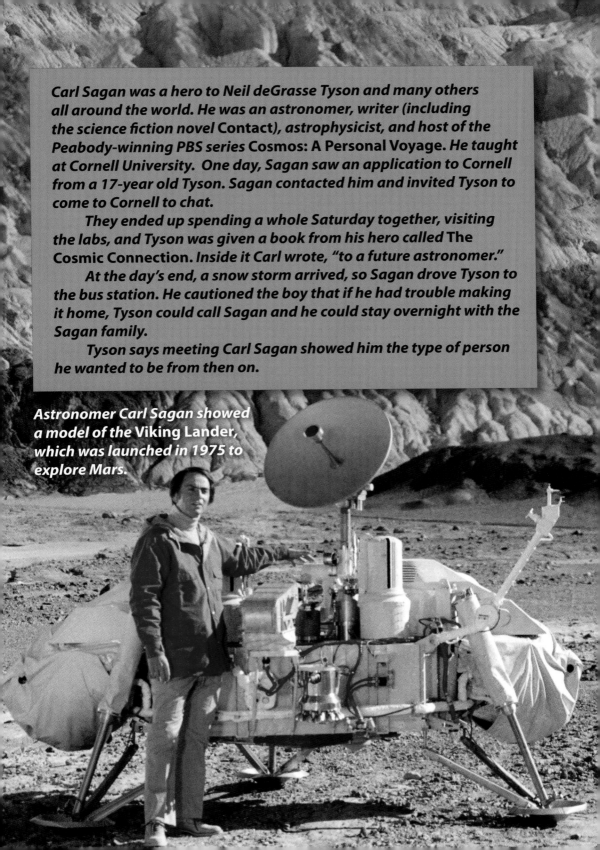

Carl Sagan was a hero to Neil deGrasse Tyson and many others all around the world. He was an astronomer, writer (including the science fiction novel Contact), astrophysicist, and host of the Peabody-winning PBS series Cosmos: A Personal Voyage. He taught at Cornell University. One day, Sagan saw an application to Cornell from a 17-year old Tyson. Sagan contacted him and invited Tyson to come to Cornell to chat.

They ended up spending a whole Saturday together, visiting the labs, and Tyson was given a book from his hero called The Cosmic Connection. Inside it Carl wrote, "to a future astronomer."

At the day's end, a snow storm arrived, so Sagan drove Tyson to the bus station. He cautioned the boy that if he had trouble making it home, Tyson could call Sagan and he could stay overnight with the Sagan family.

Tyson says meeting Carl Sagan showed him the type of person he wanted to be from then on.

Astronomer Carl Sagan showed a model of the Viking Lander, which was launched in 1975 to explore Mars.

Here are some of his tweets from 2013:

Nov. 30: That shining twilight flame? Neither saucer nor plane. Afloat in western skies, behold Venus with your eyes.

Nov. 24: If house cats were in charge, I wonder if they would post videos of cute humans doing stupid things.

Nov. 15: If Thor is strong for mystical reasons, he doesn't need big muscles. Could make him scrawny and he'd be just as powerful.

Nov. 5: If a football field were a timeline of cosmic history, cavemen to now spans the thickness of a blade of grass in the end zone.

How old is the universe? If its age were represented by a football field, the entire existence of humans would basically be a blade of grass.

Tyson even used Twitter to talk about goofs he found in the 2013 movie *Gravity*, starring George Clooney and Sandra Bullock. While he said he liked the movie, he had fun talking about the science in it:

> Mysteries of #Gravity: When Clooney releases Bullock's tether, he drifts away. In zero-G a single tug brings them together.
>
> Mysteries of #Gravity: Satellite communications were disrupted at 230 mi up, but communications satellites orbit 100x higher.
>
> Mysteries of #Gravity: Why Bullock's hair, in otherwise convincing zero-G scenes, did not float freely on her head.

Perhaps Bullock used anti-gravity hairspray on the trip.

Then he offered this thought-provoking tweet: "Why do we enjoy a SciFi film set in make-believe space more than we enjoy actual people set in real space."

His passion for promoting space exploration was still strong.

Tyson found mistakes with the science in the movie, *Gravity*, but he really liked the 2014 movie, *Interstellar*. He tweeted, "The producers knew exactly how, why and when you'd achieve zero-G in space."

Tyson is a big man with a big voice and an even bigger imagination. He collects cosmic ties and fine wines. He's a calligrapher (someone who specializes in fancy handwriting) who sometimes writes with quill pens made from ostrich feathers. He is famous enough to go to parties with celebrities, and humble enough to answer science questions from everyday people while walking New York streets. He is part scientist, part showman, and full-time preacher—because he believes there is a message to deliver and a nation to excite. He wants to restore the science energy the United States had on its 1960s quest to land a man on the moon.

Science can be fun as well as interesting and important, and Tyson sells it with nonstop charm and humor. There are so many fascinating things in the sky if you're willing to look, so many reasons to explore it if you have the passion.

Tyson does. He believes the country's future depends on it.

During a lecture at Purdue University in the fall of 2013, he said the economy needs science, technology, engineering, and math to grow. Space exploration leads to breakthroughs in many other areas.

He said scientists and engineers create solutions to problems before they happen.

For instance, the large asteroid Apophis is set to pass close to Earth in 2036. If it hits Earth—calculations show it shouldn't, but you never know—it would cause a worldwide disaster.

"That's why it's good to have you out there," he said to Purdue students. "To save the planet."

In an essay for *Parade* in 2007, he wrote that innovations that were developed to fix the Hubble Space Telescope were used to help fight breast cancer. If we don't invest in our future, while other countries are investing in theirs, he says, America will be left behind.

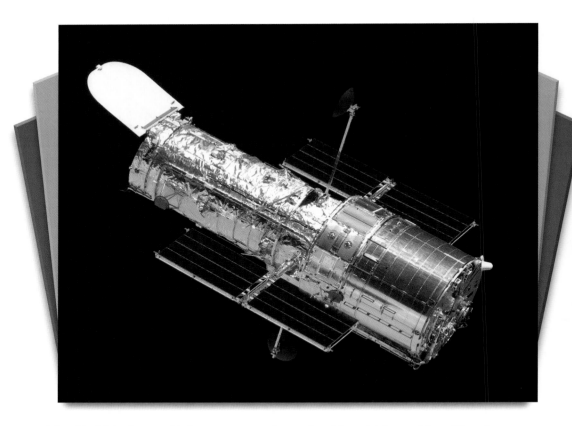

The Hubble Space Telescope was launched in 1990, and is still going strong orbiting the Earth.

The Earth is big to us, but it's tiny compared to Saturn, the second-biggest planet in our Solar System after Jupiter.

Tyson ended his lecture by reading a famous quote by Carl Sagan. While Tyson read, a large picture of Saturn glowed behind him. In the starry background behind Saturn was a blue dot.

Earth.

"Look at that dot," he read. "That's here. That's home. That's us. On it everyone you love, everyone you know, everyone you ever heard of, every human being who ever was, lived out their lives."

Each of those people is unique. That's the way it should be, Tyson said.

"I think the greatest of people that have ever been in society, they were never versions of someone else. They were themselves. . . . I think the greatest of people in society carved niches that represented the unique expression of their combinations of talents. . . . So, your task is to find the combination of facts that apply to you. Then people will beat a path to your door."

Yes, Neil deGrasse Tyson helped kill Pluto, but more than that, he teaches, creates, and inspires Earthlings everywhere.

Notes from Neil

Over the years, Tyson has written or said some very interesting things. Here are some examples:

1. On what to do if meeting an alien: If an alien lands on your front lawn and extends an appendage as a gesture of greeting, before you get friendly, toss it an eight ball. If the appendage explodes, then the alien was probably made of antimatter. If not, then you can proceed to take it to your leader.

2. On bedroom monsters: As a child, I knew that at night, with the lights out, infrared vision would discover monsters hiding in the bedroom closet only if they were warm-blooded. But everybody knows that your average bedroom monster is reptilian and cold-blooded. Infrared vision would thus miss a bedroom monster completely.

3. On McDonald's claiming to have sold more than 100 billion hamburgers: You can make a stack high enough to reach the moon and back, and only then will you have used your 100 billion hamburgers. This is terrifying news to cows.

4. On the wonder of science: It is astonishing to realize that until Galileo performed his experiments on the acceleration of gravity in the early seventeenth century, nobody questioned [ancient Greek philosopher] Aristotle's falling balls. Nobody said, "Show Me!"

5. We fail in even the simplest of all scientific observations— nobody looks up anymore.

1958   Neil deGrasse Tyson is born on October 5, to Cyril and Sunchita Tyson.

1969   Neil Armstrong walks on the moon.

1970   Tyson's parents give him a telescope.

1973   NASA launches *Pioneer 11.*

1976   Tyson graduates from the Bronx High School of Science. He is accepted at Harvard University.

1980   He attends the University of Texas and joins the dance team, which wins a national contest in International Latin Ballroom Style. He meets Alice Young.

1982   He begins writing columns for *StarDate* magazine.

1988   Tyson and Young marry. They will eventually have a son, Travis, and a daughter, Miranda.

1988   Tyson and his family move to New York City.

1991   Tyson receives his PhD from Columbia University and takes a job as a researcher at Princeton University in New Jersey.

1992   While still at Princeton, he joins the Hayden Planetarium science department.

1996   Tyson becomes the director of the Frederick P. Rose Center at Hayden Planetarium.

2000   The Rose Center opens. Tyson changes the solar system exhibit by taking Pluto out of the nine planets.

2001   President George W. Bush appoints Tyson to a committee that discusses ideas for the U.S. space program.

2004   Bush appoints Tyson to the Moon, Mars and Beyond Commission. NASA awards Tyson with its Distinguished Public Service Medal.

2005   He begins hosting the Discovery Channel series *NOVA ScienceNow,* which runs until 2011.

2006   The International Astronomical Union classifies Pluto as a dwarf planet. Tyson joins NASA's advisory council.

2009   He begins hosting *StarTalk Radio.*

2012   He "finds" Superman's planet, Krypton.

2014   He becomes the host of the *Cosmos: A Space Time Odyssey* series on Fox.

2012   *Space Chronicles: Facing the Ultimate Frontier* (with Avis Lang)

2009   *The Pluto Files: The Rise and Fall of America's Favorite Planet*

2007   *Death by Black Hole: And Other Cosmic Quandaries*

2004   *Origins: Fourteen Billion Years of Cosmic Evolution* (with Donald Goldsmith)

2004   *The Sky Is Not the Limit: Adventures of an Urban Astrophysicist*

2000   *One Universe: At Home in the Cosmos* (with Robert Irion and Charles Liu)

1994   *Universe Down to Earth*

1989   *Merlin's Tour of the Universe*

Works Consulted

Cahalan, Rose. "Star Power—Neil deGrasse Tyson, MA '83, is the Public Face of Science. But He Says His Success Has Nothing to Do with UT." *Alcalde*, February 12, 2012. http://alcalde.texasexes.org/2012/02/star-power/

Cain, Fraser. "Why Pluto Is No Longer a Planet." *Universe Today*, January 5, 2013. http://www.universetoday.com/13573/

Colombo, Hayleigh. "Astrophysicist Tyson's Lectures Are Out of This World." *Lafayette (Ind.) Journal & Courier*, September 20, 2013. http://www.usatoday.com/story/news/nation/2013/09/20/neil-degrasse-tyson-lecture/2844679/

Gary, Tonya. "Dr. Neil deGrasse Tyson—The Prodigy Astronomer." *Parlé Magazine*, n.d. http://www.parlemagazine.com/black-history-month/959-dr-neil-degrasse-tyson--the-prodigy-astronomer.html

Gibson, Kirsten. "Neil deGrasse Tyson Brings Laughter, Astrophysics to Purdue." *Purdue Exponent*, September 20, 2013. http://www.purdueexponent.org/features/article_ff708c2c-2216-11e3-990a-001a4bcf6878.html

Houston, Thomas. "Dr. Neil deGrasse Tyson on Killing Pluto: 'All I Did Was Drive the Getaway Car.' " *The Verge*, March 26, 2012. http://www.theverge.com/2012/3/26/2903224/dr-neil-degrasse-tyson-killing-pluto-on-the-verge

Louie, Elaine. "Possessed: Stars in His Eyes over a Pen." *The New York Times*, March 9, 2003. http://www.nytimes.com/2003/03/09/style/possessed-stars-in-his-eyes-over-a-pen.html

"Neil De Grasse Tyson: Sexiest Astrophysicist." *People*, November 13, 2000. http://www.people.com/people/archive/article/0,,20132902,00.html

"Neil deGrasse Tyson Trolled 'Gravity' on Twitter, And It's Pretty Hilarious." *BuzzFeed*, October 6, 2013. http://www.buzzfeed.com/adambvary/neil-degrasse-tyson-trolled-gravity-on-twitter

"Neil deGrasse Tyson to Give Free Lecture at Purdue." *Purdue News*, September 3, 2013. http://www.purdue.edu/newsroom/releases/2013/Q3/dr.-neil-degrasse-tyson-to-give-free-lecture-at-purdue.html

Shure, Caitlin. "Secret Lifer Revisited: Neil deGrasse Tyson Saves Superman." *NOVA: The Secret Life of Scientists and Engineers*, November 28, 2012. http://www.pbs.org/wgbh/nova/secretlife/scientists/neil-degrasse-tyson/show/scientist-saves-superhero-neil-degrasse-tyson-loca/

Tyson, Neil DeGrasse. "Why America Needs to Explore Space." *Parade*, August 5, 2007. http://www.haydenplanetarium.org/tyson/read/2007/08/05/why-america-needs-to-explore-space

Wall, Mike. "Krypton 'Found': Superman's Home Planet Pinpointed By Neil deGrasse Tyson For New Comic Book." Space.com, November 5, 2012. http://www.huffingtonpost.com/2012/11/05/krypton-found-superman-neil-tyson_n_2077794.html?ncid=edlinkusaolp00000003

Whitaker, Charles. "Super Stargazer—Neil deGrasse Tyson Is the Nation's Astronomical Authority." *Ebony*, August 2000, pp. 58–62. http://books.google.com.au/books?id=BdkDAAAAMBAJ&pg=PA60#v=onepage&q&f=false

On the Internet

Hayden Planetarium, "Neil deGrasse Tyson Profile." http://www.haydenplanetarium.org/tyson/profile

"The Most Astounding Fact," Neil DeGrasse Tyson, TIME interview, YouTube, March 2, 2012. http://www.youtube.com/watch?v=9D05ej8u-gU

Neil deGrasse Tyson,

http://www.imdb.com/name/nm1183205/

NOVA: *The Pluto Files:*

http://www.pbs.org/wgbh/nova/space/pluto-files.html

NOVA: *The Secret Life of Scientists and Engineers:* "Neil deGrasse Tyson: Astrophysicist."

http://www.pbs.org/wgbh/nova/secretlife/scientists/neil-degrasse-tyson/

StarTalk Radio.

http://www.startalkradio.net/

Twitter: Neil deGrasse Tyson.

https://twitter.com/neiltyson

YouTube: "Neil deGrasse Tyson: My Man, Sir Isaac Newton."

http://www.youtube.com/watch?v=danYFxGnFxQ

GLOSSARY

asteroid—A small space object made of rock and ice.

astronomer—A person who studies the universe beyond Earth.

astrophysicist—One who studies the motion and forces between the stars and planets.

comet—A space object made of ice and small rocky particles that develops a long gas tail when warmed as it approaches the Sun.

congress—The lawmaking part of the U.S. government.

dissertation—A well-researched paper written to get a doctoral degree.

dwarf planet—A very small planet.

gerontologist—A person who studies aging as it relates to society, biology, and psychology.

gravity—A force that attracts objects to one another.

Hubble Space Telescope—A very large instrument launched into orbit in 1990, used to make amazing discoveries and take amazing photos of space objects many light-years away.

light-year—The distance light travels in a year, which is about 5.88 trillion miles.

Milky Way—The name of the galaxy that holds Earth's solar system.

NASA (National Aeronautics and Space Administration)—The U.S. space agency.

planet—A non-glowing space object that orbits a star.

red dwarf—A very small star that seems to glow red.

Saturn—The second-largest planet in the Solar System after Jupiter, and the sixth planet from the Sun; it is known by the bands of rock and debris that orbit it.

sociologist—A person who studies human relationships, behavior, and culture.